DISCERNING WITH THE HEART

GUNILLA NORRIS

Discerning *with the* Heart

PRAYING *for* GUIDANCE *and* VISION

TWENTY-THIRD PUBLICATIONS
twentythirdpublications.com

TWENTY-THIRD PUBLICATIONS
977 Hartford Turnpike Unit A
Waterford, CT 06385
(860) 437-3012 or (800) 321-0411
www.twentythirdpublications.com

Cover photo: stock.adobe.com/Laura Pashkevich

ISBN: 978-1-62785-814-4
Printed in the U.S.A.

A division of Bayard, Inc.

To pray is to dream in league with God

ABRAHAM JOSHUA HESCHEL[1]

CONTENTS

SUGGESTIONS FOR THE READER

This is not a book to read straight through. Let it be the kind of book that you open at random in a day, and let what you read on that page speak to you. Too many of us make work out of trying to do the right thing when, if we are truly present, we will act naturally. Something will feel more right than something else. There will be a lightness about it, in both senses of that word.

At the end of each reflection there are ways for you to wonder that might prove useful. The I that speaks in them is not me per se but a way I could imagine a person mulling the reflections to make them more personal.

If you have time, dwell on one or another of them as it strikes you. If you use this book often, you'll come back to issues that are more relevant to you than others. You'll be amazed how the book just seems to flip open to what could be of use to you. Trust that you are not alone in your process. God's love is closer than your breath. Your inner tuning will strengthen. You will be more able to stay open in conflictual situations so clarity has a chance to emerge. You will grow to be more honest about your hidden agendas, and you will be given the passion to act as a loving person in the world.

INTRODUCTION

I am struck by what Meister Eckhart wrote: *All beings are words of God.*[2] To me that means not only that our lives must speak but that we must speak as we live our lives. But to speak with any depth means to be in the school and practice of discernment, and that is not easy. We each have so much history and socialization that we rarely speak without something of those influences being in our words. Awareness and prayer are needed to help us align so that we *dream in league with God*, as Abraham Joshua Heschel put it.

To want to write about discernment has come to me through witnessing the Quaker practice of taking time to hear all sides of an issue, to dwell in indecision and discomfort with patience, to seek answers from solidarity with others and from being deeply with our own process as we try to be faithful in our lives. Every day we are discerning what seems the right way to move both in small domestic choices and in deep, heartfelt ways.

Praying for discernment is a constant task. The need for prayer shows up in countless ways. We pray because we know we are creatures who are dependent on our Source, the wellspring of our being and belonging. We pray for help with our failings and concerns, our confusions, our pains, and our gratitude. We pray to reach out to the Mystery that gives us days and possibilities for guidance. Our hearts need to pray, to fully be with Being and to grow to be more conscious and considerate in our dealings with ourselves and with others.

We are vulnerable. We are more precious than we know. We are flawed. We are creative and destructive. We are infinitely loved. To feel the truth of this is to open our hearts to the task of unfolding prayerfully. It is to grow in a relationship to our Maker, to belong in ways so profound there are no words for it. This belonging is a gift we are given outright. But the experience is realized by giving our being back to the Giver, one choice at a time. We often find the way best when we pray.

I hesitate even to use the word "prayer." There is much overlay for me with that word. Questions about who or what God is—as well as questions of religious preference and authority—come up, all of which tend more to separate us than to unite us. I grow silent. Perhaps you do, too. God for me is a mystery. I can say nothing about God other than that God *is*. I use words like Source, Spirit, Life, Love, the Sacred, and Reality interchangeably to stand for that Mystery which is unnameable.

Praying comes in as many forms as there are human beings and in as many issues that life presents us with. There is no end to this, but there are constant beginnings. What you will find here are small reflections on discernment followed by prayers. For me, prayer is sometimes silence, sometimes words and longing, sometimes confession and regret, sometimes sensing with the body, and sometimes simple action. My hope is that you will dwell on the subject and come to your own words, actions, and prayers. I hope you will mull and wonder.

It's very difficult to define what discernment is. My experience tells me it is not a process of judgment—this is good and that is bad—though judgment can point me in a direction that allows me to see what is preferable. It is not analysis, either, though gathering information, even on the fly, can serve the discernment process. It is not merely the mind that is involved. My feelings are, too, and when I really dwell with discernment, my body wisdom has a voice. How does all this work together when decisions have to be made almost in an instant? I can't answer that except to say that for me, discernment is fundamentally prayer, a habit of turning within to the relationship with the Divine of my inner being and asking for guidance.

I don't think I am alone when I share that as a decision is discerned and is aligned with love, then a curious and subtle release happens in my body, a feeling of being held into the flow *with* life even though I know difficulties will accompany what I chose.

We have habits, good and bad; we have longings; we have dreams; and we need to discern to live conscious lives. That means we are always beginning. I describe some ways to be about discernment here that may be useful, but I believe it is prayer that helps the most and makes us humble and open to Divine guidance, putting us into an inner listening that is individual and also holds us accountable to a *will* greater than our own. I hope that as you read, you will find your own way of approaching discernment and ways to pray so it is your heart that leads the way.

Discerning
with the
Heart

Not Finally
in Our Hands

When I am faced with two choices that seem polarized in my thinking, I *short out*, not unlike an electrical wire that is no longer able to conduct the current. The coupling of two different wills to one action can send up sparks. I can see the difficulties and the merits of both sides. I am reluctant to choose one at the expense of the other. I may even want to live both. I may want to avoid other people's disappointment or judgement because I want to choose one thing in favor of another, which I know they would not prefer.

In cases like that, we may either not have the courage or not have the wisdom to discern a proper course. Most likely we haven't the trust and the patience to endure being confused and in conflict.

Our praying then perhaps needs to be about accepting discomfort and yielding to it, giving it time so both sides may be heard fully. We need to pray for a quality of presence that is without judgment.

Discernment and judgment are often thought to be the very same. But discernment simply reflects as a mirror does, whereas judgment colors what we see with opinions. A discerning statement might be *That is a wool sweater.* Judgment would say, *That is an ugly wool sweater.* In judgment, we often resort to opposites. This is good. This is bad. This is better. This is worse. And in the presence of such judgments we often feel diminished or inflated since neither is a truthful reflection. In discernment, each thing can breathe and so find its proper place. It is not a matter of either/or but one of both/and. So often our minds balk at that.

The time it takes to listen and to reflect is an embodied prayer. It takes time to hear what our gut has to say. It has a deep wisdom, a knowing beyond that of the ego mind. We find that kind of wisdom most surely in the body. Such knowing is not only realistic but also completely truthful. It is my experience that the body never lies.

Faced with two choices, I like to place one in my left hand and the other in my right hand. Then, with both choices held in my hands with equal respect, I try to find a prayerful space inside where I can be neutral for the moment.

I might turn to God with these words (if you try this, use words that you like better):

May I make room for all of this.
May I feel You listening with me
in the midst of all this.

I like to write down or even speak out loud the pros and cons. I can listen with my entire body. It takes time to listen and sense until I feel that all that is in my left hand has been reflected and duly noted.

Then I repeat that process with my right hand. Finally, I join my two hands together very slowly and offer up the whole dilemma to God. I may pray with these words, but you might prefer to use others:

I release the tension of not knowing to You.
This choice is not finally in my hands but in Yours.

I give You my willingness to be led.
Bring me to a faithful choice.
Allow me to see the way.

I have found that to simply proceed with something ordinary, like washing the dishes or making the beds, which has nothing to do with the issues, is a good way for a resolution to come to me. By simply moving on, I often find that the choice is silently made within me. It will feel somehow *right* and I can be at peace with it.

Taking Note

When was the last time I was in a situation of having to decide between two equally important things? Can I remember how that felt? Was it exciting or fearful? How did I rush myself in the process and do what seemed expedient to get off the hook? Is there a pattern I can see? How do I duck knowing what I know?

Can I think of times when I gave myself more time to decide when I was under pressure? How did I handle the frustration and the discomfort? In retrospect, would I have chosen something different? How hard am I on myself about that now?

If I regret those choices now, can I turn them over, knowing that mistakes anyone makes are also used in God's big picture? I know I am to live now, not back then. I long to trust myself more and live more daringly. This needs to be in God's hands, too.

Praying When We Must Choose

C larity implies light and focus. To bring in more light, we adjust the telescope or the magnifying glass to be able to perceive clear outlines and a refined resolution. We may expand the lens to take in more of the background or the foreground. But even with more information, we may not be any the wiser.

This often happens when we are choosing among good things that seem equally good. Or it may happen when we choose between unavoidable evils, trying to discern which is less harmful. Sometimes we are in situations that are neutral. It doesn't seem to matter what we choose. In those moments, recalling ourselves to the presence of God brings a different perspective. We might be able to forgo our own lens in order to see. Our prayer then may be a simple question:

What is Your way for me here?

Some questions demand specific answers, and others are more like wonderments. I find the latter to be more useful, for this brings me first and foremost to my relationship with God. When I wonder out loud with God, I am asking for God's perspective, allowing my own to be at rest for the moment. This does not mean permission for me to skip the effort of having to work at discernment. I so much need to feel that I am not alone in the process.

Sometimes what we need is not clarity. It may not be lack of knowing but the weight and responsibility of knowing that weighs on us. We may then pray the question:

Will You be with me in this?

In the foggy nights of the soul, when it is inwardly both dense and lightless, simply stopping and knowing that just now things are very murky is clarity enough. Then not being able to do or see anything *is* the way. We may only be able to reach into further uncertainty, Braille-ing forward, feeling every step of the way.

Then our words might be these or others like them:

I am lost. I do not trust my own way.
Yet You are trusting me with this.
May I be worthy of Your trust.
Even as lost as I feel, help me to go forward.
May I be lost in You.

DISCERNING WITH THE HEART

Taking Note

There is nothing wrong with not knowing. Will I allow myself a little time to simply not know? What makes me hurry up so much of the time? Where do I think I am going? Am I just picking up the speed at which information is coming at me on the computer and the TV? Who says all of this has to be digested?

Everybody is not good at everything. Could I allow someone I trust to help me think things through? Who could that be, in this case? I know that just naming things with a witness by my side has an effect. Am I secretly ashamed that I can't keep up? Perhaps just asking for help will be a help. For hundreds of years, the cry for help has been understood to be part of being faithful. That's a comfort.

Why is it so very important for me to be right? I'm in the school of life, and I'll only graduate at the very end. Mistakes can be the best ways to learn. Can I remember that when I make a mistake, it might just be a good thing?

Praying
for Clarity

Clarity is both limiting and expanding. It asks us to be aware of what is actually happening, what we are feeling, and where we realistically are. This requires truthfulness and acceptance. By acceptance I do not mean approval but a willingness to surrender my denial or at the very least to own that I am in denial. It may also mean for me to give up living on treasured hopes in an idealized version of reality.

Clarity is work! It makes us real persons, humble and ultimately beautiful. It is an asceticism which, when willingly and even joyfully embraced, forges our integrity. Let's admit it, clarity is mostly forced on us. Difficulties just happen. We are stopped by an unwillingness or inability to integrate the difficulty. At those times we are thoroughly reminded that we are only creatures after all, and of short duration at that.

But what if disruptions, frustrations, misadventures, and disappointments are invitations to suffer willingly, and here I use the word "suffer" in its old usage, *to allow*. To allow the truth that there is horror, meanness, mixed motives, greed, and all manner of difficulties that we cannot control and that often were set in motion long before we were even born. How do we find clarity then?

For me, prayers of surrender and yielding at least get me to the truth that I am not able to see the whole picture. I am and we are creatures who are far too limited. We can live our little puzzle piece, our precious fragment, with as much integrity as possible. That is all. Limited, confused, even blind, we are nevertheless part of possibility.

The image of a tree has helped me here. Its bark sets limits. Its root system stabilizes the tree and locates it firmly in place. The circumstances are, in a way, arbitrary. Why was the seed blown to this place? Why did it fall just in that spot, and why were the circumstances right enough for an initial rooting? These are questions that can't be answered with certainty.

Yet, the tree does root down and grows because of its roots' inherent ability to do so and because its sheathing bark protects it. Slowly the roots of the sapling inch down, and later the stem reaches up and out. It is the limits that make the tree possible. Ring by ring it becomes more. This applies to us as well. When we are stopped, stumped, confused, irritated, enmeshed in all those constant frustrating moments when there is no clarity, could we simply use a question as a prayer?

What is enough just now?

Could we voluntarily surrender our urgency to solve the whole problem? Could we turn to the Source of possibility? We will usually get enough clarity for the next little while: something simple that can be lived at the time. But we might also be told that enough is to wait. That's all, period, until something beyond our knowing can change. We might have to pray the question again and again and receive nothing but silence.

What is enough just now?
What is enough?

To live this way can give us clarity for just this minute, a clarity that is both sharp and double edged. It may limit us and open us at one and the same time. We can grow to trust small God-given answers for the moment's need, the moment's truth. In the grace of such limits, we will grow by inches, and in time we may discover that we have branched out and have a full view of the sky.

Taking Note

When Jesus said, "Suffer the little children to come to me," he meant *allow* the little children. So much pain comes to us because we don't allow what is true in the moment. Could I allow myself to be innocent, open, young? Am I afraid of being seen as childlike?

Why do I have to be smarter than I am when it's okay to be smart enough for now? When did I start expecting an unlivable standard for myself? Besides, there are all kinds of smarts. Some of us can be great at numbers, organization, and promotion. Others are wonderful healers, helpers, and teachers. God made me good for something, not for everything.

What if I rooted down into the soil of how things exactly are and trusted that more will come clear in God's time? Everything isn't up to me. Instead of working at being so responsible, could I just be response-able? That might actually be fun.

Sorting
What to Live

D aily, there are so many opportunities we can lend ourselves to. We can be pulled here and there, into this and that, simply because it is there. Sometimes this leads to a vague sense of being lost in muchness. Or we can stubbornly deny that we have as many opportunities as we do have and cling to old habits and to people that do not serve us and that we allow to keep us from growing.

Just because one is a good cook does not mean that one's primary work in life is to be a chef. Or just because one was not a good student in high school doesn't mean there are no opportunities now for success in something one loves to do. Our minds can chatter and tell us almost anything if we do not pause, if we do not question, if we do not seek our answers from the love of God within us.

The mind does have the capacity to will a moment of recollection. It is important to know that the mind is not only a seducer, a fountain of rationalization, a wellspring of countless irrelevant ideas, but that it can also serve as a guardian and a warrior on our behalf. The mind can learn to act on the heart's behalf. When we use our minds to stop and question, the heart has a chance to open and receive answers. Then we might hear the guidance from our deepest nature, the soul God gave us.

We don't want to know how easily seduced and taken off the path of our heart's true longing we can be. The immediate wants and the momentary satisfactions pull us greatly. This is well illustrated in many fairy tales. The hero or the heroine has a task to perform in order for restoration and wholeness to happen. He sets out and is soon offered lovely jewels, clothing, fame, and whatnot, which pulls him away from his true task. He falls asleep or is trapped in some way and so forgets his purpose. This is folk wisdom. These stories, whether about men or about women, tell us that we forget who we are, and that it is the plain gold ring of wholeness that must be chosen above all else.

The paradox is that it is with the mind that we learn to stop the habitual responses, the automatic seductions, and the alluring bewitchments that the mind produces. The mind can learn to focus on the heart. It can give the heart that breathtaking moment to pray its question.

Is this mine?
Is this mine to live?

It seems the answer comes most usually in a body knowing, a body hunch that speaks a clear *yes* or a clear *no* or throws the question right back at us to ask again and again until we feel the way we must go. When the body and the soul are aligned, we can hear from a different level. We are in*formed*.

It is very hard to trust that we are so deeply loved and known by God that we are trusted with our particularity. With such trust, we are able live in an open state of questioning. We don't have to have all the answers. We can continually ask for clarity. To be the persons God gave us to be, we cannot live everything. We must live what belongs to our nature. Then daily and many times a day when we are offered opportunities, we can seek to align with God's purpose for our unique being. We can pray the question:

Is this mine?
Is this mine to live?

Eventually, over time, the question is not so much consciously asked as felt by the body and lived by the soul. With our minds supporting our hearts, our hearts will grow ears, and we will live by prayerful listening.

Taking Note

When was a time I heard my essence speak with authority and I followed through? I want to remember how aligned and hopeful I felt. There was no doubt. There was a simple knowing, a felt sense of something being right. I want more of my life lived that way, and I will pray to become aligned with my core.

What are the situations when I seem to be deaf to my core? What is behind that deafness? Fatigue? Boredom? Laziness? Fear? I want to know what triggers me. Sometimes the triggers are big, sometimes they are subtle, but they will almost always have the same root ... be it a need to be in control, a need to be loved, a need to be safe or a need to change what is going on. I need to stop long enough to sense what controls me.

There's a difference between what I think should be mine and what really is mine. The former is some kind of ideal image; the latter is vital and truthful. Can I let go of ideal pictures of myself and live the vitality of what is true? How afraid am I to be real, to be what God wants me to be? Being what God wants me to be will no doubt feel like freedom. I'll be living what is mine to live.

Clear in the Freedom of God

To be truly human means to know that we are always in ambiguous places inside and out. We will be revealed in our frailties. We will be standing hip high in our mistakes. Looking closely at any of our actions, there will be self-preservation, self-serving, and self-importance mixed with love, courage, service, devotion, and humility. Being human is a mixed bag. This we can be clear about.

So, seeking clarity in order to be good or to avoid blame, or to guarantee our safety and comfort, will not help us in the end. We will always find ourselves with dirt on our hands of one kind or another. The welter of the world will not stop. We will always be mortal, vulnerable, and human. We will be humus, part of the earth.

When my children were growing up, we would sometimes go rock hunting. One day we were finding garnets in an old mine site. It was amazing to see perfectly formed crystals embedded in a schist of indifferent gray stone. We knew the schist was what allowed the crystal to form in the first place. Being human is a bit like that: the essence is often held in murky matter. We are jewels in dirt.

When we give up being right, perfect, and blameless, we can give up the burden of so much self-concern and become interested in what is happening in us and around us in the moment. Then, when the going gets rough, we will not be so self-protective. We will have a broader concern. We might very well want to pray:

What serves life here?

This prayer helps us get away from what only serves our own purposes or the tendency to please someone else's personality, which we might do to avoid being faulted by them. Instead, if we ask what serves life, we are lifted from the constraints of personality and so can readily sense how we participate in a bigger context. Many of us are aware of people who take their convictions as true gospel and then politicize their private opinions. When we ask what might serve life, it must be taken as a question that includes the good of the whole, not just one small faction with which we are aligned. We are in the freedom of God, and that is what makes us persons. We have value, not of our own making but of God's gifting, and that gifting has made us varied. Accepting that diversity is, in fact, unity, then even in small, seemingly unimportant decisions we can set ourselves to one side and ask to find freedom in a prayer such as this:

What serves life here?
What serves the whole?

Often, the worry about being right or blameless or safe will fade a little to the background, and we will be better able to stand in the moment's light, the moment's gift, the moment's wonder. It is there that the love of God is present, and it is there we can take our next step.

Taking Note

A vacation from myself? What a concept! What new possibilities are mine now? To what am I drawn if I don't have to prove anything? What will happen if I pay attention to my heart's leanings? Will my life change a lot? Will I feel safe enough?

How refreshing not to *have to be* right or to do the right thing. Does anyone really know for sure what is right? Maybe there are many ways to be right, depending on the situation. How much more can I notice of what is around me if I give up the notion that there is only one right way at any given time?

Do I dare act on the idea that when I serve life instead of just myself, will I experience satisfaction and freedom? Will it feel different from just doing what I want? Will I be empowered to live from a deep authenticity? Do I dare? Do I dare?

The Field of Forgiveness

Most days, we are likely to miss the mark in small and sometimes very big ways. Most of us do our best, and more often than not we discover that our best is limited. This can be searing on the one hand and liberating on the other. We can stop kidding ourselves about our great virtues and be human instead—that is, to have the grace to know that all of us are in need of forgiveness all the time. Our capacity for right action and unconditional love is not a constant. It seems to disappear more often than it appears.

All of us have non-acceptance days. We don't want to know or feel the truth of our condition. We don't want to apologize or change our actions. We are in a closed system—a negative day.

Sometimes it even feels good to feel bad. We label ourselves irredeemable for the moment and so can stop struggling.

Everything can go belly up for all we care! This vacation from trying our best doesn't last very long. Those days soon get to be boring because they are fixed and static. We tend either to up the ante of our dark mood to feel even worse, just to create some action, or we flip to the other extreme. With heroic, unrealistic expectations we resolve to be better than better.

We need the discernment to ask for forgiveness when we are caught in circumstances such as these. We might recognize that we are giving allegiance to images of who we are or who somebody else ought to be. Unconsciously, we are demanding reality to be as we think it should be, or we deliberately make it out to be worse than it is. We are praying to gods of our own making: Shame, Blame, Ought, and Should, the unforgiving gods.

Sometimes using an image can be a prayer and may help us. If we can turn our eyes away from our current separation from love, we can turn inward instead. There we might allow ourselves to experiment, to imagine spaciousness—a meadow, perhaps, with tall grass and no boundaries. We might imagine it to be the heart's great field, with room for everything. If we can get past our inner stone walls, we will find that the field beckons us, waits for us, and invites us to move into the open. This generous field never comes to an end. We can walk into it forever and discover that it has no boundaries. It is the given-ness of everything—excluding nothing. It is God's generosity, which is *for* us and *for* everyone.

This is everybody's field. We are invited to wade in and to pray along with the whispering grasses.

That, too. That, too.

In God, whatever it is that needs acceptance, there is space for. We might not immediately be able to include hurtful events, but in the unending expanse of the heart's field, there will eventually be room for those, too. The very distances can help us be inclusive. The heart of love has boundless acreage, with room and time for it all. Already it embraces everything, including our lack of forgiveness.

It is in God's *given-ness* that we live. That given-ness is *for* us. When we enter the heart's field, we can know that all of us are already forgiven. In time, we can grow to accept more of such radical reality. We might learn to whisper like the grasses in the wind, including more and more into our hearts.

That, too. That, too.

Taking Note

This reflection is nice and poetic, but really how can an image help? I'm sure we've been told that we carry unconscious images inside. If that is so, can I spend some time thinking about what negative images I have of myself that show up without my permission? Probably I won't like what I find, but starting there I may see the sense of how such an image might affect me. Let me start a list. *I'm not good enough. I'm special, so I should get lots of attention. You have to work for everything you get.* etc.

Maybe there is something to having space for absolutely everything, even whatever negativity I discover in myself. At least that spaciousness is democratic. I wonder what would happen if I spent a whole day letting all the things I encounter simply belong—even the ones I don't like?

Being in nature is almost always healing. It's not hard to imagine a huge field, but believing that it is inside me is another matter! But if I could imagine it as there, I would have a place to put things my mind can't handle yet. Saying *That, too* would be a prayer in which I let things go, let them flow into the field and not have to track them. *That, too* would be my turnstile, my gate to more space.

Releasing
Judgment

Releasing Judgment is not a tabula rasa. We have had many experiences growing up. Some have made us sensitive and reactive. Sometimes we don't see things clearly but as though through a scrim, a veil. Perhaps fears of a psychological nature arise from the ways that our parents, teachers, and contemporaries treated us when we were young. Some children are continually assessed, their performance and their appearance scrutinized. That may have been lovingly intended by the parents in order to protect the child in the future and to prepare the child for adult life. Very often these parents were assessed in similar ways when they were young. We tend to teach what we have learned, even if it was painful to us. When standards and expectations are impossibly high, we cannot measure up; the result is a feeling that we cannot be loved unless we are perfect. Sometimes we expect that from our families, friends, and even members of our worshipping communities.

To be so evaluated and judged, whether positively or negatively, tends to put us in a box. It is as if the flowing, moving film of our lives is stopped at a particular frame and we are trapped in its image, unable to move on. We may look to see how others react to us and try to find our reward in living up to their expectations. Or we live safe lives, taking few risks. Then we are organized around avoiding criticism and responsibility.

Growing up with assessment is very common. It will skew our discernment. Not one of us escapes it entirely. Learning what is expected, what we should and ought to do, is necessary, but when we are too much exposed to assessment and judgment, our lives become about performance and goals and not about joy. We will be slaves to that ever-renewing, ever-present bottom line and often hold others to it as well.

Our image of God can also become that of God the Judge. We must *earn* heaven. Love and grace are not free and present gifts. They are down the line after we are perfect, a state which we never reach, for more judgments arise and we are caught in frame after frame of being *not quite right*.

How do we pray when we are boxed in by judgment and box others in it, too? No words will solve this, for our conditioned minds will find yet newer, better ways to reach for that illusive perfection that promises release. The judging eye is like a glaring spotlight, and we are deer stopped in our tracks. We become our own or someone's target stripped of our natural, spontaneous movement. This may take the internal form of self-incrimination, or plans may arise for *how to deal next time*, or we may run incidents over and over in our minds in helpless repetition. We plan what we are going to say or do.

We must dare to leave the mental trap of assessment the very moment we discern that we are trapped in it. To move is one of the simplest, most human things we can do. This is not absurd. Our bodies can walk us out of the mind's glaring spotlight, taking one simple step after the other without any concept in mind. Our lungs are constantly filling and emptying. We are *in* movement all the time. This is organic. Without movement there is no life. We do not need strategies or ingenuity or expertise to take a step and then another. Though we may not have immediate solutions for our fear of judgment or of our judgment of others, there is life available outside of fear. By moving, we can more readily feel this.

Each time we are trapped by judgment, we can choose to walk a prayer. Let us remember that God is not the God of Judgment but the God of Life and Permission. Whether we walk a long way or a short one, let us sense that life in God's permission always is a movement towards love. As we walk, we might sense words like these:

*I am trapped again in judgment
or in another's assessment of me.*

*I ask to feel your Presence.
May I walk in Your love and permission.*

*May each step move me
through fear into life again.*

Taking Note

I won't sneer at suggestions that seem too easy. They probably are not; they are just assessed by me that way. Okay, then, let me take up movement when I'm scared, angry, or confused. It would be a blessing to stop words for a bit. Someone told me once that if I let myself shake all over for a full minute when I have an upset of any kind, this will help. If I also make whatever sounds I want to make, like "Brrr," that it will help. It's worth a try.

~~~~~~

There are judgments made of me by others that hurt more than other judgments. I do this to me, too, of course. What if I could stare down those thoughts and words, let them be just words and thoughts, not the gospel. Everybody has a ding or two. What if I just agreed without getting in a huff and said, "You're right. So what?" That would be a change. It's worth a try.

~~~~~~

It's strange that whether an assessment is positive or negative, it's still an assessment and puts me in a frame with a label. I either have to make up for a perceived inadequacy or keep trying to be better than better. I wonder if God doesn't love our faults as much as our triumphs. If a rhino is as precious as an ant, there's got to be worthiness for each one of us. Maybe we can strut our stuff with a little more freedom? It's worth a try.

Letting Love into Fear

So much of our life is run by fear: remembered fear, anticipated fear, immediate, present fear. Reluctant to entirely trust the moment's possibilities or the people around us, without even knowing it we have our guard up, ready and mobilized. We certainly do not look like we are doing this as we go through our days, but it doesn't take much for the alarms to go off and for our distrust to be operative. We call it many things, from precaution to common sense. It is simply true that part of our evolutionary inheritance is to be ready to protect ourselves. Our sympathetic nervous systems are wired for fight, flight, and freeze. This is so ingrained, we are not aware of it. Like nation-states, we operate with much of our budget allocated for defense: some 100%, some 70%, some 50%, and a lucky, trusting few at 10% or less. Even if this is true, there is a central aspect of our humanity that does not want to lead life remembering, anticipating, or engaging in defense against danger and pain. We sense, deep down, that we are meant for love, freedom, and self-expression.

Unknowingly, most of us are bound by early, unconscious decisions we made when we were small and not prepared for life. Ways we were treated and events we had no control over become silent blueprints in our being. We learn early to defend against our defenselessness. These decisions over time become habits of being. They are part of our personality traits, revealed in our bodies, in our movements, in the way we fully breathe—or not. In short, they are the scripts we live.

But we are intrinsically open systems that are meant for love and self-expression. So, most of us do the best we can and don't think about this much, though we can feel the tug, that longing for freedom, for something more fluid and trusting.

To return to the intrinsic possibility God places in us takes enormous courage and deep yearning. Experiences of grief, of anger, of discouragement, of ill health and depression remind us of our lost potent selves. In a strange way, these states of being are love seeking to be remembered. How paradoxical it is that embracing what is wrong with a loving attitude and understanding will help us step into what is right! We were not meant to merely cope. We are meant for fullness of life.

But we cannot will these changes. The bootstrap methods soon falter. It doesn't take much time to find that such strategies are merely new defenses. They are work and not grace. We must let God into our fears. How do we do this?

With discernment, we can learn to be willing to know what triggers us. Any repeated emotional or physical discomfort is a messenger. Say we are easily irritated, on the defensive, persuaded against our best interests, or spaced out. We can begin to notice when this happens and how frequently it shows up in us. These attitudes are messengers that tell us we feel threatened. To hate the messenger means we will not hear or understand the message. *Something needs love here.* Without attention, and by default, we create concrete bunkers of isolation. We will be more locked in than we were before.

With God's help, we can learn to embrace the messenger, for then we might each come to know the early threat to our young psyches and remember our deep birthright to be whole and free. We can learn to turn inward, letting go of self-blame and the blame of others. We can move through our fears and surrender our vulnerability to the Source of love. We can receive God's gift of life again and again. Daily we can know that we are re-created by God and that our essence is good—*very good.*

Often we cross our arms over our chests when we feel threatened. Could this gesture become an embrace instead of a shield? Instead of holding ourselves in rigid protection, could we be proactive and hold our shivering selves with compassion in God's presence? Could we pray words like this:

May I feel You with me when I am this afraid.
May I have the courage to understand what
memories and habits hold me hostage.

May I learn that my fears are messengers, not enemies,
and that I can begin to treat them kindly.
With Your love, may I embrace myself.

In everything may I turn toward You.
I receive my life daily, knowing that it is good.
May the courage to live fully be mine again.

Taking Note

What a heady conviction to have that God re-creates every one of us daily. We get to be the same old and yet new each day. What a deep invitation that is! Can I let go of my same old just enough to feel what is new and potential in me today? With my morning coffee could I sense into what is new. Or at least ask to overcome my reluctance. A sip at a time, let me ask to welcome what is new.

※※※※※※

In my head, I know having fears is human; nevertheless, I want to push any discomfort off my plate. Really feeling vulnerable is scary to me. But it is the place I can be met. My resistance is not me. Love wants me as I am—tears, fears, and all. Can I also want me as I am? That is what is new and something I can move toward. Will I risk being that real?

※※※※※※

A hug a day keeps the doctor away: a new mantra. I will hug myself today a few times and also open to being held not only by Spirit but by those who care about me. I want to practice letting love in, allowing a little love to light-shine into the deep, fearful parts of me. That will always be new.

The Switch from Guilt to Remorse

When the capacity to forgive or to be forgiven appears to be stalled, a hidden refusal might be the reason. We may think we *should* be able to receive forgiveness or to give it, but in fact our feeling state is dark and secretly unmoving. It is as if there were an electrical short inside us. Our thoughts and feelings somehow cancel each other out. No light goes on when we flip the desired switch.

This may be for many reasons, one of which might be the confusion between guilt and remorse. We sometimes say, *I feel so guilty about that*, when we want exoneration for something. Or we might say, *So-and-so should feel guilty about what they did*, when we think we want to forgive but cannot. Guilt is a curious state. Feeling guilty, we may think we *ought* to do or not do something, but our actions do not align with our thinking. A deeper level in us is full of resistance. Then our actions speak for us instead, and we behave as if we were saying, *I am doing what I am doing (or not intending to do) anyway!* We cannot square our image of ourselves as good persons if we are direct about our deeper intentions. Feeling guilty or inducing guilt in another is like throwing a bone in the maw of our *shoulds* and our *oughts* while proceeding right ahead with our intention.

When we feel guilty, there is no true self-alignment in our behavior. We are a house divided. Our lights are out. We can neither fully enjoy what we are doing nor stop what we believe we shouldn't do. We just keep throwing that guilty bone over our shoulder while we keep everything just as it is. Most often we are unaware of what we are doing because it is below the surface of discernment.

When we induce guilt in another instead of offering an openhearted attempt at forgiveness, we have a deeper motivation. We want the other person to be in emotional debt to us. We want the power of being *in the right* and better than the person who disappointed us or betrayed us. When this is the case, we bind ourselves further into continued betrayal and disappointment. We keep alive the very thing we say we want out of our lives.

Remorse is very different from guilt. At the heart of remorse is a willingness to change, to set things right. At the heart of guilt is an unacknowledged refusal to change. It is a state in which we want to remain in the dark, in control, or at the very least on hold.

Caught in these very human traps from which we cannot extricate ourselves on our own, we may need to pray for the light of discernment. What if we could designate one of the light switches in our home, one that we turn on often, to be that prayer symbol that will hold us to the task of turning toward remorse when we fail others or ourselves. Whenever we throw the switch we might remember to pray:

May Your light so fall into my being
that I might see myself clearly without guile.

Help me to not act as a judge
or one that is being judged.

Help me to relinquish feeling guilty.
Help me to resist having to be right
or the obsequiousness tendency
to make myself wrong.

Help me feel and know how equal
is everyone's need for exoneration.
May remorse be my motivation for change.

May I live in Your freedom to change
and to grow in love.

Taking Note

A light switch: What nonsense is that? Praying with a light switch—how can that help? Maybe staying with a simple thing for a long time has some effect. I turn the kitchen light switch on and off lots of times a day. Could I really ask for help each time the light goes on? Could I stop guilting and start changing? How many times of switching will it take, I wonder?

The desire to be justified is really the desire to be right and have no one pointing the finger at me. I don't want to be less than anyone. I don't want to be less than my best opinion of myself either. That's a stalemate. Nothing can change. It's like wearing shoes two sizes too small. Maybe if I do ask light to come into these dark corners of myself I will be helped. It won't be up to me entirely. At least with actual light being shed, then inner light may also be felt. I'll keep notes.

I need to remember that I'm not alone and a special case. Everyone is in need of help. Knowing that might be a way to share in humility. Can I turn that light switch on not just for me but for us? Can I pray for freedom for everyone who is boxed in like me when I am unwilling to be honest and vulnerable?

Leveling the Mind

What would happen if we perceived our ignorance and fallibility and the ignorance and fallibility of others to be an invitation to love? Wouldn't we be less likely to shut the doors to our hearts and minds? We would sense how rampant is the communal need for compassion and forgiveness. None of us are exempt from this need. It is one of the most stable facts of human life. Having such an understanding can level us. We are not exclusive cases. We are all persons in need of forgiveness and also ones who can look out at the world, recognizing how equally we share that need. It is a democratic condition.

We share the world and we share its pain. We also share forgiveness. The release of even one of us is that much release for the whole. Everything is so vitally connected to everything else that any deep forgiveness work any one of us does benefits the rest. Whether we receive forgiveness or give it, or whether we simply stand by and witness it in the lives of others, we are partakers. It is here we can learn to be in the discernment of the heart instead of in the mind's ideas of what is right and wrong.

Being relentless about being in the right (and we all have our exclusive take on that) divides us. Being in the heart brings us to God together. This is a leveling process. When a builder uses a level, he is seeking a perfect horizontal line. In the tool's viewing glass, the little bubble settles in the middle when things are level and true. When we are level with each other, the heart is like that balance point, and yet it ranges out in a horizontal way to include more and more, even that which we cannot immediately see or know. Releasing our separate and exclusive claims, we find ourselves in God's constant, inclusive forgiveness. No one is less deserving of it, and no one is more deserving of it. God's love is a level for us all.

To be leveled is humbling. Generally, our egos do not like to give up the demand that we have a special status in the world. But being leveled is not diminishment. It is rather a straightening, a horizontal alignment with others. When we open up to our inability to forgive, we discover that we are, in fact, on the playing field with everyone else. God's love goes out to all of us, and all of us are in need of it. We are equalized by it. Then we can realize how very lonely it is to be unforgiving.

Though we cannot forgive on our own, we can do our part by putting ourselves in the possibility of that grace. Could we be truthful and level with God? The more we understand how wide and endless God's love is, the more we might be willing to extend ourselves also, to abandon hierarchy where one thing or person might be forgiven and not another. Could we pray a *being willing to be willing* prayer?

May my heart extend to the horizon.
May I not be afraid that my failures
cannot be forgiven.

May I offer up my need to hide.
May I be empty of judgment and feel
how necessary is God's love to us all.

May I be willing to receive God's forgiveness
and also the forgiveness of others.

May love make me willing to be willing.

Taking Note

I like to think of the horizon as that place where sea and sky or plains and sky meet. They morph into each other. It's hard to tell where one begins and the other ends. But looking at things vertically, you can see what's above and what's below. I think judgment is about putting things into above or below, whereas compassion stretches far beyond what can be seen. I want to live horizontally, inclusively. When I feel a judgment coming on, I will look far out instead of up and down. Let me keep track.

The heart thinks differently from the mind. While the mind tries to figure out solutions and to be done with things, the heart wants to be present and to listen. When the heart is in charge, that desire to be present is a very strong pull. It is a willingness, a form of will that is simple and about availability. Can I learn to listen to my heart so I can listen to what matters? With both feet on the ground, aren't we leveled? Without solid ground, how could I live? Facing the horizon, and with my feet on the ground, I am just a little pip-squeak that is learning to learn. I want to remember there is nothing wrong with that.

Differences among us are wonderful, but I want to also think about what I have in common with others. The need for forgive-ness and compassion, for sure, is one. The time to figure things out not just by myself but with others I can trust is another. Letting go of perfection is a third. We can only do our best, and that has to be good enough. Can I see others doing their best? Can I acknowledge that I often try to do my best? It's hard to be judgment free, but maybe I can keep remembering that every-one actually tries to do their best most of the time.

Belonging to Limits

We can only be the ones we are. We can only live in the time we live: the day, the hour, the minute, the second. Our minds and spirits can soar into the limitless, but it is within limits that our lives are forged.

Can we learn to fully rejoice in limits without falling into discouragement? We say, *She is a limited person. Such-and-such has limitations.* What if we could see limits as structure—that limits can lead to furthering, to development, to growth? This requires discernment and acceptance of what is possible now. We rejoice when an infant has learned to grasp a rattle. We don't ask a child of three months to be able to stand and walk.

The discipline of a Zen meditator, taking a firm, unmoving seat in front of a wall, is a powerful image of someone working with limits to transcend them. We can cook because the lid is on the pot and the pot is squarely on the burner. We accept that premise without question. It is much harder to accept what is happening to us when we are on the burner and the heat in our lives is turned up.

Limits can be lived and endured if we discern that they will help us progress rather than if we sense they will constrict us. A musician is able to practice hours and hours of scales because he wants to play a sonata so well that it melts the listener's heart. But many are the times when there is no seeming progress, only more frustration.

For most of us, it will not be hard to find the occasion and the subject of our prayer when it comes to limits. All we need do is sense the common frustrations we have. We can feel we are in the pot with the lid on, and the burner has turned red. It is precisely there that we can discover and seize the moment and see it as a glowing opportunity.

If we could imagine there was a pause button right in the middle of our chests, we could place our hands there and press in gently. We would learn to use a pause touch to remember that we are not alone. God is with us even in our difficult moods and unloving responses. Pausing, we might use these words or others of our making:

Here I am again
revealed in my lack of acceptance.
Be with me.

I am stomping and stopped in mid-plan.
Be with me.

I cannot discern how this situation benefits
anything or anyone.
Be with me.

I feel diminished in this and cannot be
the one I want to be.
Be with me.

I am not enough for this.
Be with me.

Taking Note

We expect a lot of ourselves. We expect a high standard to live up to (and sometimes we expect the opposite). Often, we don't even know it is we who are putting the pressure on or excusing ourselves. Without limits, we are probably not able to see our hidden agendas. They tend to be both subtle and variable. This time I can goof. It won't matter. Another time I'll have to be on the rack if I fail. There's something inhuman in these standards and the credence we give to them. I haven't thought of myself as inhuman when I pressure myself. Can I begin to notice?

I think setting a reasonable limit on the efforts of a day is the beginning of being human and taking care of our nervous system. Small, doable goals make sense. Challenges that are the right size are fun. The ones that are too much make us too little. Even the machines we use daily have stop mechanisms or pause and idle buttons. I will think of such a button being in the center of my chest. When I heat up too much, I will put my hand near my heart and whisper, "Please chill." Enough really is enough. I need to practice believing that and see if my body feels better when I treat it humanly.

I'm noticing that when I access a slower pace and reasonable limits, I actually get more done. I don't have to recover from the exhaustion of too much. I have the limit of my skin, my given physical structure, my age. Those things count, don't they? When I am 85, I will not run a marathon, but I may watch one with someone I love. Taking stock of what my true limits are will be a recognition that I am a creature, a human creature, not made for everything but for some things that fit and are God-given invitations to me. Let me pray to know what those are.

Embracing Our Inner Selves

No matter how tough and shiny our exteriority might be, we are all vulnerable inside. There is a malleable, sweet softness at the core. To belong to our inner selves, we need to love our essence and be in solidarity with it. It is in our core that we find our connection to God and to life itself.

I amuse myself by thinking of this as an M&M matter. We are all a melting sweetness behind glossy Teflon shells. To belong to our inner selves and therefore to God, we need to be accepting of the fact that our shells are necessary. We need them to set limits. We need them to be safe and capable enough to take care of our needs.

What is not necessary, though, is a continual polishing and further layering up of our shells. We can certainly discern that the ego mind has the needed function of proper protection, but having a hard and shiny ego is not our purpose. Our purpose is to be the one we are at our core and so to discover our life in God. Then we will naturally melt out and our lives will be of satisfaction to us and of sweetness and service to others.

Many people cannot distinguish their ego mind, their shell, so to speak, from their vital essence. It is all one to them. But there is a telltale method to discern the difference between the two. Most of us will find that when genuine tenderness is extended to us, we feel ourselves melting. Our automatic protection is momentarily suspended. We are gentled somehow and can both be and let be.

To want to belong to what we are at the center, which Quakers call *that of God* within us, is an intrinsic, human longing whether we have words for it or not. It is simply basic. How do we pray our way there?

There are as many ways as there are people, of course. One method I use often with myself and have taught others over the years has to do with using my hands in prayer. First, I find a quiet spot and a quiet time to be with myself. Then I bring my awareness to my hands. I imagine (think/sense/feel) that I am putting tenderness into the open palms of my hands.

As I do this, I ask for God's tenderness to be there as well and for the ability to feel it. I cup my chin with my hands, the way a grandparent might cup the face of a beloved grandchild. Then I say with all my being:

May tenderness be in my thoughts.
May tenderness be in my perception.
May tenderness be in my speaking.
May tenderness be in my hearing.
May I be cradled in God's tenderness.

I move my hands to cover my heart. I say with all my being:

May my heart be filled with tenderness
toward all the good in my life.
May my heart be filled with tenderness toward all
that is difficult in my life.
May my heart be open to my fears and regrets.
May my heart be open to my confusion and anger.
May God's tenderness be the welcome
at my heart's door.

Now, I move my hands to cover my belly just below the navel. I say with all my being:

May my stability be strong and soft.
May I never be outside of God's tender holding.
May I be cradled in love.

Done over time, this prayer begins to move from the shell to the core. Often, the words fall away, and the placement of the hands becomes a silent petition. The felt longing in the gestures grows into tenderness. We may discern that we are *already* in the hands of Love and that it is *already* established in us.

Taking Note

It was in Africa where the "heart touch" was taught to orphaned children who had been traumatized. Placing our hands on our hearts confirms not only that we have hearts but that we can give solace to ourselves and receive solace from others and from God. It is so simple to do, so present and direct. I want to do this every day in solidarity with others. We are an earthly family. We need each other's hearts and to claim our own. I will think of the best time to do this every day.

ffffffff

I know when I am polishing my ego because it is full of effort and makes me feel alone. I'm busy trying to be more than I am, and in the end I don't believe in what I have polished after all. It feels off. In the process, I haven't really been with anyone, including myself. The need to polish just makes for more need to polish, and then loneliness grows. Tenderness seems to be the best way to let go of ego-insistence. We are meant to have a heart, aren't we? We need to be touched by tenderness a little every day, starting today.

ffffffff

Our hands can do so much. They can destroy. They can heal. They can create and they can express love. With my hands in front of my mouth, I want to breathe love into them and become conscious of how I use my hands throughout the day. I want to dedicate them to right use. The symbol of two hands together is the symbol of being at prayer. But what if being aware of the way my hands touch everything in my life could be an ongoing prayer? I know that to touch with tenderness and to be touched by it has power.

*With*dom

I nternally asking the mind to be silent is a beautiful and needed thing to constellate conscience. The heart isn't loud the way the mind is. Stillness lets the heart speak. That is why silence is given so much importance in all spiritual traditions.

Once the heart has been heard, the mind can add ideas of how to implement the heart's wisdom. We need for our minds to serve our hearts, not the other way around. The mind changes all the time. It may tell you to get a pizza with the works one moment, and then as you are eating it may say, *I wouldn't have done that if I were you.*

The mind roams, it concludes and approves and then forgets what it decides and does something else. The heart is another matter. Even unconsciously it is connected to Spirit. *That of*

God cannot be erased from it. The heart knows and feels in a different way than the mind.

When the mind serves the heart, discernment is possible. That is, conscience becomes possible. I don't mean conscience in the way we usually think of it, the one that is authoritative—a superego that shames and guilts. No, conscience is from the Latin, *con scientia*, "knowing with." When the mind serves the heart, it thinks *in concert with* the heart. It's not a loose cannon anymore. I've coined the word "*with*dom" in other writings. Discernment is really *with*dom.

We always need another in the process of discernment. We need each other the way the heart needs the mind. Alone and without references to anything or anyone else, we have no perspective. We are only fully human together. The African word *Ubuntu* says it well: *I am because we are.*

When a team acts together, they are more likely to win, but whether they win or not, they have something of great value: namely, respect for the contributions that each member makes. This is bonding energy that can be felt.

We have a mind and a heart. They do not always act together. With the lack of this bonding, we live at sixes and sevens. Someone observing us could easily spot that we are lost, without purpose or direction.

How do we come to an inner place from which to act with discernment and conscience? The answer is together. First in silence so that we can listen to our hearts. Then by allowing the mind to join the heart in *with*dom. And lastly by reaching out with respect and a recognized need for each other.

Before I act, may I quiet my mind.
Before I act, may I listen to my heart.

May I allow the mind to inform me
but not force me or repress me.

Before I act on anything of importance,
may I ask for reflection from trusted others.

May I always listen to the Spirit first.
May I be led to act with conscience.

Taking Note

To be and act independently is held as a good thing by many. To stand on our own two feet, make and carry out decisions with our wits and grit is the hero's and heroine's way. That is a pronounced myth in Western culture. But isn't it true that we are both a *we* and a *me*? We are in life together. This is hard to keep in mind when I make a decision. If what I am about to do is good for me, will it hurt someone else? It's a question I need to ask often.

First things first. In deciding something important, may I first listen to my heart enough to know whether what I desire is a true desire or just passing fluff. Why act unnecessarily, just because? Second, do I have some idea what the expense, time, and energy will cost to act on my desire? Third, will my decision hurt others? These are all discerning questions. They take time and awareness. They ask something from me before I go pell-mell into whatever has drawn me. If something is important, then I have to give it importance. More notes to make!

It is comforting to talk things over with someone trusted. To ask for someone's *with*dom not only honors them but honors us as well. We are each worth a thoughtful hearing, both in giving our attention and in receiving attention. I long for the deep decisions I have to make to be made with love for myself and with love from a friend. This is not about wit and grit but about being response-able together.

A Blessing Way

What if we could cease making strangers of ourselves? So often we create circles of estrangement. We live on *us* and *them* terms. When we do, we not only make strangers of others but inexorably we make strangers of ourselves. Everything that *is* is life now and belongs to life. Stating that something should not be or must not be, even dreadful things, separates us from the depth and mystery of existence.

To be human, we must admit it all or be condemned to be strangers. This, of course, does not mean we should suspend common sense in caring for ourselves and those in our keeping. But it does mean deep acceptance and acknowledgment (I do not mean approval) of both terror and beauty, nastiness and hunger, grace and bereavement, hatred and love.

Being inclusive this way disturbs our ego minds. We want to be safe, look good, and stay in control. We want to be undisturbed. All of us know this well. It is almost automatic in us, which means we lose what is human in us to something mechanical. We live from habit and without discerning choices rather than out of blessing.

I have never been able to tackle this deep-seated tendency in myself head on. I don't think any of us can do this successfully. It is too deep a habit structure. But I do know that, though we are not changed so much by reformation, we can be transformed by reconciliation with the profound generosity, permission, and love of God. Our automatic parts do not need restraint. They need restoration, to belong and to be blessed.

What seems necessary here is to suspend, even if only for a moment, both discernment and judgment. Yes, we do assess and discern all the time, and we need to do it to manage our day-to-day lives. There's no disputing that. But if, for a moment, we could dismantle our immediate *separation* response to threat and turn to blessing instead, we would be safer and less estranged in the world.

Doesn't the sun shine on the just and on the unjust alike? Doesn't the rain, when it falls, water our common ground without discrimination? Why not copy this kind of blessing?

We are all familiar with the phrase *random acts of kindness*. Let us consider *random acts of blessing*. Imagine that every time we are in judgment, every time we are out of the circle of belonging, we might find a way to silently pray, beginning with ourselves. Buddhists call this way of praying *Metta*. The traditional words used may be different from ones I am suggesting here, but the intent is largely the same.

> *May I not make myself a stranger.*
> *May I find blessing instead of judgment.*
> *May I be restored to belonging in the world.*

Then, turning to the object of our displeasure, we could pray:

> *May I not make you a stranger.*
> *May I know that you belong.*
>
> *May you be blessed.*

This might be condensed into much simpler phrases:

> *May I feel that I belong.*
> *May you feel that you belong.*
> *Together may we find blessing.*

This process takes only an instant of our time, but practiced for months, it disposes the heart to realign with the world through belonging and care instead of distrust and rejection. We can then perhaps grow to feel that everything belongs and is necessary, though we might not discern why, and that it has the possibility of turning into blessing.

Taking Note

We hear "bless you" when someone sneezes. Long ago, it was thought that the soul left the body for a moment when someone sneezed and had to be blessed to find its way back. That's not a bad idea that can be enlarged. Starting each day by blessing the coming hours and encounters will help me be aware of how close grace actually is. It takes less than a minute and can change the tenor of the day. Let me not forget this ancient practice.

In slower, more rural times, there were often blessings made when lighting the first candle of an evening, drawing water and at the ending and beginning the day. We have kept some of that practice by blessing food and each other at significant events such as baptisms, weddings, and other solemn occasions. But to bless everything we touch and interact with is different. We consecrate the daily in small acts of remembrance. It will naturally make us more discerning. When something is intrinsically respected, it is a blessing. How much I need both to give and receive blessing.

When someone says "Bless you" and means it, warmth is there. That blessing reaches further than we can immediately know and feel. Could it be that if we silently bless persons and situations that are difficult, they can be transformed somehow? At the very least, practicing blessings in those circumstances will keep me out of judgment. I won't be adding to the pain that already is. With a habit of blessing, I might find a freedom I never would have dreamed I could have.

Receiving God in Everything

"God" is a word that we use and whose meaning we think we know. But in truth, God is always far beyond our understanding. We can only know God by unknowing. Through love alone do we take God into our being. The anonymous author of the medieval text *The Cloud of Unknowing* puts it this way: *By love God may be gotten and holden but by thought of understanding never.*[3]

We *get* and *hold* only by giving ourselves over in longing and devotion. Whether in action or in quiet stillness, it is the simple, direct emptying of our selves in love-longing that opens the door for God. And then we may catch glimpses of God's presence everywhere and in everything.

Since love-longing is a gift from God to begin with, placed inside us *before always*, as C.S. Lewis put it,[4] we yearn for God because God yearns for God's Self in us. Our part is to bring our small, human will fully to this yearning, to become that willingness, that living devotion in whom God is returned to God.

We can participate in love not so much by feeling but by discernment and choosing to align ourselves with what God has placed within us. Feelings come and go. We are up one day and down another. The world calls us in countless ways, and we cannot help but have feelings about anything and everything. That is not so important. What is important is our constancy. Constancy is based on daily choice. No matter how we feel, when we light the wick of our willingness, we say *YES* to love. New light emerges. The deepest part of love is willingness. It is our most precious gift.

Offering our willing *YES*, day after day, moment by moment, in joy and despair, in seeming boredom and intense participation, in resistance and in action, in stillness and exuberance, we will surely be transformed. We will be united not only to our own core but also to Life itself. In time we will experience that we have been and are held in God's being all along. We will understand that our persons and our lives are lived prayers.

May I know that, as I wait for You,
You await me.
May I choose to give myself to the longing
you have placed within me.

May I trust that through such yearning
I will grow to know You.

May I become entirely willing
and give myself fully to Your love.

Taking Note

Though our feelings fluctuate and aren't always constant, we can nevertheless keep turning toward being constant in our devotion. In some Buddhist traditions, a period of meditation can be dedicated to a person or a situation. Why not dedicate a day to being constant in our will to turn toward God as our center? We'll have lapses for sure, but intention is a very powerful thing, and a repeated intention can be astounding. A simple prayer of dedication at breakfast done over and over has a way of penetrating our core. That minute a day can set our compass for life. Even a week of trying it will have an effect.

❧❧❧❧❧❧

The will to be constant is answered by God's constancy. We are not alone with our puny wills. To know we are wanted by Love itself can fuel us and create in us a vibrant intention to live in communion with the Source of our being. Then both joy and difficulty, grief and mercy will be so intertwined that we are made robust enough to live all of it fully.

❧❧❧❧❧❧

Things don't have to be the way we want them. In our constancy, we can discover that what is given us to live is precisely what we really need. We may not like this at all. Discerning the truth of this will take time. But what a relief to receive our circumstances as avenues of creativity, growth, and ultimate wholeness. It is in daily prayer that we keep turning our will to God's will, and in so turning "we come round right" as the Shaker song "Simple Gifts" so beautifully puts it. This way of living may become effortless effort in time. Can I give myself to this? What simple, doable intentions and actions am I willing to engage in "to come round right"?

CLOSING

Spontaneity in prayer is wonderful. Our spirits rise and flicker like flames. We are warmed with enthusiasm and bright with possibilities. But there are days when we are dry, tired, discouraged, numb. We all know a steady fire requires tending. Without constancy, the fire goes out. We are left with ashes. It is in months of steady prayerful discernment and focus that longing becomes belonging. Our prayer life isn't real until it is reliable. We must give ourselves to it to find ourselves. When we do, we will discover at our core an undefended opening to be loved as we are.

What is left to say? Perhaps because it is still winter and the season of Lent as I write this, I want to share an image of what prayer feels like to me now. If it is anything, it is like walking in a vast snowy field, a field without end. Anyone traversing a snowy field in blazing sunlight knows that the world seems magnificently illuminated, and at the same time it is so bright, one is blinded by it. This field is an open invitation that lies before me each day. There are no footprints. The surface is undisturbed, and I must just step one more step into that mystery which is both entirely luminous and utterly dark.

Sometimes I can turn around and look back at my tracks and see how I came to be where I am. But they are old tracks. They fill in or they melt. The field still always lies ahead, ever opening. Again and again, I have to discern and decide to take that small next step that seems to be the right one at the time. As the novelist E.L. Doctorow said, *It's like driving a car at night. You never see further than your own headlights, but you can make the whole trip that way.*[5]

The ways of praying I have shared in this book are footprints I have taken. Of course, not all of them at a time. If you find even one such step in the process of discernment to be of value for you, I would rejoice. I am sure you know that whatever way inspires you to be in prayer must be continued for some time. When we take a train, we don't change trains at every stop. We would never arrive at our destination. If by simple liking or by curiosity you find some way to pray that I have suggested, then make it your prayer for some time. Stay with it. I assure you that it will change organically.

Your way may be to pray with words, silence, gestures, intentions, or specific actions. But the way the spiritual life usually goes, we will at some point find ourselves in that vast field where only God's companionship is reliable. For even as we try to discern ways to be with God, God has been about discerning within us from the beginning. Psalm 139 puts it well.

Oh Lord, you have searched me and known me.
You know when I sit down and when I rise up;
you discern my thoughts from far away.
You search out my path and my laying down,
and are acquainted with all my ways.
Even before a word is on my tongue,
Oh, Lord, you know it completely
You hem me in, behind and before,
and lay your hand upon me.
Such knowledge is too wonderful for me;
it is so high I cannot attain it.

We must trust that God deeply discerns us and loves us. Our journey will no longer be so much a journey *to God*. It will be more a journey *in God*. Our own efforts are small compared to God's effort on our behalf. And sometimes we will have to let go of what has sustained us in the past. Doing so, we will no doubt feel lost and vulnerable.

Only our willingness to daily discern with God's help how to live allows God to move in us and to guide our lives. Each step, whether in terror or in joy, in contentment or in doubt, in dread or in confusion, will move us closer to home. Then it is God's love that finally takes us over the threshold.

For I tell you this,
one Loving, blind desire for God alone
is more valuable in itself,
more pleasing to God
and to the saints, more helpful
to your friends, both living and dead.
than anything else you can do.
THE CLOUD OF UNKNOWING[6]

ENDNOTES

My gratitude goes to my wonderful library friend, Beth Hanson, for her work in verifying the sources of the quotes in this manuscript.

1   Abraham Joshua Heschel, "Prayer," in *Moral Grandeur and Spiritual Audacity: Essays*, ed. Susannah Heschel (New York: Farrar, Straus & Giroux, 1996), 353.

2   Meister Eckhart, "Expands His Being," in *Love Poems from God: Twelve Sacred Voices from the East and West*, trans. Daniel Ladinsky (New York: Penguin, 2002), 112.

3   *The Cloud of Unknowing*, introductory commentary and trans. Ira Progoff (New York: The Julian Press, 1957), 72.

4   C.S. Lewis, *Perelandra* (New York: Scribner, 1996), 183.

5   George Plimpton, "E.L. Doctorow: The Art of Fiction No. 94," *The Paris Review* 101 (1986), 299–313.

6   William Johnston, ed., *The Cloud of Unknowing* (Garden City, NY: Image Books, 1973), 60.

ALSO BY GUNILLA NORRIS

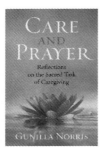

Care and Prayer
Reflections on the Sacred Task of Caregiving

In this beautiful and profoundly helpful book, Gunilla shares reflections from her experience as a caregiver that offer hope, strength, and support for each day. Suffused with real-life wisdom and deep spirituality, *Care and Prayer* is a light-filled companion for full-time caregivers, or anyone involved in caring for another.

96 PAGES | $12.95 | 5½" X 8½" | 9781627855662

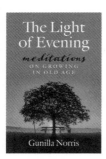

The Light of Evening
Meditations on Growing in Old Age

"Sometimes in quiet moments I wonder, how did I get to be this old?" A must-read for anyone entering the second half of life, *The Light of Evening* reminds us that aging offers the unique opportunity to wake up to what really matters and embrace the freedom and grace of living in the light of God's love.

112 PAGES | $14.95 | 5½" X 8½" | 9781627857024

Great Love in Little Ways
Reflections on the Power of Kindness

Is there anything more needed in our world today than kindness? In this little gem of a book, Gunilla helps us learn to cultivate kindness in all aspects of our daily lives. *Great Love in Little Ways* is a book to savor and read over again as it broadens our awareness of God's kind and loving presence in today's sometimes harsh and chaotic world.

96 PAGES | $12.95 | 5½" X 8½" | 9781627854290